Greeting Cards
using Digital Photos

Greeting Cards

using Digital Photos

18 step-by-step projects for uniquely personal greeting cards

Cheryl Owen

Martingale®
& COMPANY

Martingale® & COMPANY

Martingale & Company

20205 144th Avenue NE

Woodinville, WA 98072-8478 USA

www.martingale-pub.com

Senior Editor: Clare Sayer

Production: Hazel Kirkman

Design: Gülen Shevki-Taylor

Photographer: Shona Wood

Editorial Direction: Rosemary Wilkinson

10 09 08 07 06   10 9 8 7 6 5 4 3 2 1

Reproduction by Pica Digital PTE Ltd, Singapore

Printed and bound by Times Offset (M) Sdn Bhd, Malaysia

Acknowledgements

Special thanks to Annette Claxton, Dorothea Grimberg, Catherine Holmes, Catherine Hughes, Alex Lattes, Corinne Masciocchi and Clare Sayer who generously lent photographs and to Shona Wood for the beautiful photography.

contents

Introduction

Greeting cards are exchanged throughout the year either to mark a special occasion or just to say hello. Making a hand-crafted card shows the recipient just how much you care. Lovely creations can be achieved quickly and easily either by incorporating a craft technique you already enjoy or by experimenting with a new one. Using photographs to make greeting cards will bring a smile to someone's face as you remind them of a favorite occasion or person, or gain their interest as you share a precious moment or a scene from your travels. If you enjoy digital photography, you will certainly have a wealth of photos to choose from to create some stunningly original greeting cards.

All the projects in this book are suitable not only for digital photos but those on print film too. If you use print film, use a matte print or have a photocopy made. The basic techniques are explained concisely and there are full-size templates at the back of the book to ensure a professional finish. Let the projects inspire you to put your photos to creative use where they can be enjoyed and treasured by many people.

DIGITAL PHOTOGRAPHY

When a digital photograph is taken, sensors capture the image and convert it into a series of electronic pulses which are compiled into an electronic file for storage in the camera. JPEG, GIF, BMP and TIFF are some of the formats for storage. Digital cameras have a slower reaction time than film cameras as they acquire information before a shot is taken. For action shots, pre-focus the camera on something close to where the subject is expected so the camera will respond quickly.

A digital file can be opened on a computer with an imaging program such as Adobe's Photoshop. Use these programs to manipulate the image too, such as by changing the size or background color. Once you are happy with the image, it can be printed onto paper ready to make into greeting cards.

Pixels

The word 'pixel' is abbreviated from 'picture element'. Digital images are composed of thousands or millions of pixels. Most digital cameras offer 2-5 million pixels. The more pixels, the better the image.

Memory

Photos taken with a digital camera are stored in a memory which is an arrangement of silicon chips that record information like a computer. Most cameras have 'card format memory'. The cards can be removed and replaced quickly which allows many photos to be shot without having to return to base to download them.

Downloading photos

The easiest way to transfer photos from your digital camera is to connect the camera directly to a photo printer, although this will only give a paper record of the images you have taken. The more versatile method of saving digital photos is to connect the camera to a compatible computer and download them. If you store the images on your hard disk drive, bear in mind that they take up a lot of disk space. Always keep a back-up copy on CD. Alternatively, store the images on CD. When the images are saved on your hard drive, use the computer's file manager to show a list of files of your images.

TOOLS

Although you do not need a lot of special equipment for cardmaking, it is a good idea to equip yourself with some good basic tools.

Drawing

A mechanical pencil is best for accuracy as it does not need sharpening. An HB lead is the most useful for general drawing and a softer lead such as a 2B is recommended for transferring images. Use a ruler and T-square to draw true squares and rectangles. Make sure you have a good selection of felt-tip pens and marker pens for decorating your cards. Include some silver and gold pens and gel pens as they are very effective on colored papers.

Safety Tips
- Always work on a well-lit, clean and flat surface.
- Keep sharp implements beyond the reach of children and pets.

Cutting

A craft knife or scalpel is essential for cutting straight lines. Craft knives are better than scissors for cutting cardstock because the card is kept flat while cutting. Rest on a self-sealing cutting mat when using a craft knife or scalpel and cut straight edges against a metal ruler. Replace the blades often; a blunt blade will tear the surface of paper and cardstock. Take care when changing the blades and dispose of them sensibly as they are very sharp.

A craft knife can also be used to score cardstock so that it folds neatly. However, a bone folder, which is a traditional bookbinding tool, is best for scoring because it dents the foldline rather than cut it. Bone folders are available inexpensively from paper suppliers and craft shops.

For best results, use scissors that are comfortable to handle – a sharp pair of general-purpose scissors is most useful. Cut small, intricate shapes with embroidery scissors but be aware that paper can dull scissors that are intended for use on fabric.

Pinking shears and decorative-edged scissors cut paper with a shaped edge. Paper punches are available in various shapes to punch decorative holes in paper. The punched holes can also be stuck decoratively to a greeting card or used to make confetti. Sequin shapes or confetti can be slipped into a greeting card to surprise the recipient when the card is opened.

Pierce small holes with an awl or a thick needle, resting on a cutting mat. A stationer's hole punch makes a precise hole quickly. Snip wire and fine metal with wire cutters or an old pair of scissors.

Painting

Use good-quality artist's paintbrushes for painting; a fine and medium round brush are the most versatile. Always clean brushes immediately after use. Paint can also be applied with a rubber stamp or natural sponge.

MATERIALS

A huge range of materials can be used to create your greeting cards, from delicate Japanese papers to paints, ribbons, sequins and beads.

Paper and cardstock

There is a wonderfully inspiring range of paper and cardstock available nowadays. Art shops and specialist paper shops have colorful papers from all over the world. More unusual varieties include embroidered papers and handmade papers incorporating petals, leaves and fragments of textiles. Handmade papers are often expensive but a single sheet will make many greeting cards.

Fine Japanese papers, tissue paper and translucent papers will show the colors underneath them. There are also papers embellished with glitter or punched with decorative holes. Create your own unusual surfaces by stitching on paper either by hand or

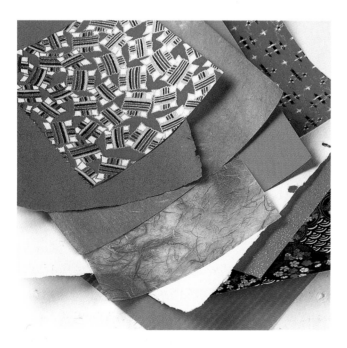

Use a variety of colored and textured papers

machine or applying paint, felt pens, glitter and inked designs with rubber stamps. Consider giftwrap, wallpaper and origami paper if you want a patterned surface. Other patterned surfaces can be downloaded from the internet.

Stationers often sell single sheets of writing paper in lots of different colors and textures. This can be an economic way of buying a small quantity of paper with envelopes to match.

'Gsm' indicates the weight of paper measured in grams per square meter. The larger the number, the heavier the paper. Good quality paper produced especially for photographic purposes is available in packs of 25-100 sheets. It usually has a glossy coating on one side. For photographic prints 240gsm weight paper is recommended. Photos can be printed on ordinary printer paper which is usually 80-100gsm but the quality will not be as good.

Laser printers give the highest quality prints but color versions are usually very expensive. An inkjet print is a practical alternative but make sure you print on good-quality paper, as inkjet printers can smudge on cheap paper.

Cardstock comes in different finishes such as pearlescent and metallic. Corrugated cardstock is inexpensive and comes in many colors. Alternatively, paint corrugated cardboard from packaging.

Adhesives

Always read the manufacturer's instructions and test glues on scrap paper to be sure they are suitable for the job. Use spray adhesive to glue layers of paper and cardstock. Always spray in a

Decorate your cards using paint, glitter, sequins, beads and other embellishments.

well-ventilated room and protect the surrounding area with lots of newspaper. Smooth the layers outwards from the center. Spray adhesive does not adhere immediately so you have time to reposition pieces.

All-purpose household glue is quite strong and will hold many materials. It is best for glueing small areas as it does not spread evenly over a large surface. Use paper glue in stick form to adhere lightweight paper such as inserts in place. Double-sided tape is a clean, neat way to join paper and cardstock. Adhesive foam pads have been used in many of the projects to attach motifs so they stand out from the background surface. Use low-tack

masking tape to hold templates and work temporarily but check first that it does not tear or mark the surface.

Paint

Acrylic paints are very versatile, the colors mix easily, they are quick-drying and non-toxic. Glitter paints are fun to use: tiny metallic particles are suspended in glue which dries clear. Apply the glitter with a paintbrush or squeeze it through the nozzle of its plastic container. Relief paint is also applied through the nozzle of a plastic container; it gives a three-dimensional effect. A colored ink pad and rubber stamps create an instant design feature.

Mixed media

It is often the small embellishments that make a greeting card special. Sequins, beads and gemstones add a touch of glamour. Sequin dust is the tiny holes punched in sequins, it looks like large particles of glitter. Gemstones are available with adhesive backs which makes them easy to apply. Buttons and lace will give an interesting change of texture. Wire is available in different thicknesses and colors from bead and craft shops. Stickers come in all sorts of shapes and colors and they are easy to apply. Join motifs to a card with metal paper fasteners or brads. Finish cards with pretty ribbons and cord.

Decorate envelopes that will be delivered by hand to coordinate with the greeting card. Consider how to pack a greeting card that has three-dimensional decorations, especially if it is to be sent through the mail. A padded envelope lined with bubble wrap will give protection.

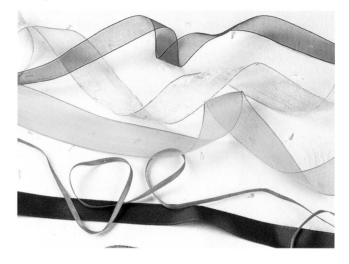

Ribbon and cord in varying thicknesses

TECHNIQUES

The basic techniques for making greeting cards occur throughout the projects. Read the instructions for a project before you embark upon it and try out new techniques on scrap materials first. Use metric or imperial measurements but not a combination of both.

Using templates

Trace the image onto tracing paper with a sharp, soft pencil, drawing straight lines against a ruler. Use masking tape to tape the tracing face down on your chosen paper or cardstock. Redraw the design to transfer it (see left).

If working on a dark-colored surface, designs can be transferred by slipping a piece of graphite transfer paper face down under the tracing then redrawing the design to transfer it.

If you intend to use a template often, maybe to make a series of cards, glue it to thin cardstock with spray adhesive before cutting it out. This will make it more durable.

Enlarging and reducing templates on a photocopier

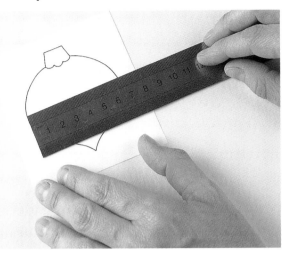

A photocopier will enlarge or reduce a motif quickly and accurately. It's easiest to work in millimeters, but if you don't have a metric ruler you can still do the calculations; just convert inches to decimals. First, decide the width of the image you want to end up with, for example 3½ in. (90 mm). Next measure the width of the original image, for example 2½ in. (65 mm). Divide the first measurement by the second to get the enlargement percentage; in this example, 140% (138%).

Enlarging and reducing templates on a grid

To enlarge or reduce a motif by hand on a grid, tape a piece of tracing paper over the original design with masking tape. Draw a square or rectangle over the entire design and divide it up with a row of vertical and horizontal lines. The spacing will depend upon the size and intricacy of the design. None of the designs in this book are particularly complex so keep the lines about ¾ in. (2 cm) apart.

Draw a square or rectangle of the required finished size to the same proportions as the square or rectangle on tracing paper. Divide it into the same number of vertical and horizontal lines. Redraw the image working on one square or rectangle at a time (see below left). Then view the design as a whole and redraw any areas that do not appear to 'flow' well.

Using a craft knife

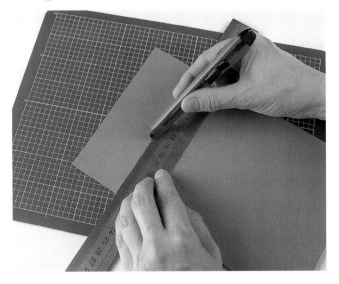

Cut straight edges on paper and cardstock with a craft knife or scalpel against a metal ruler, resting on a cutting mat. When cutting cardstock, do not press too hard or attempt to cut right through at the first approach; it is easier and more accurate to make several light cuts until you cut through.

Folding cardstock

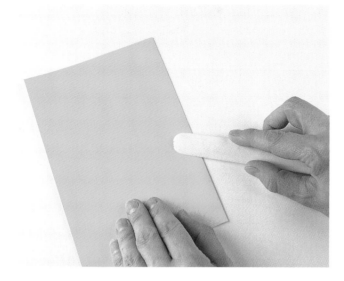

It is easier and neater to fold cardstock and thick paper if a fold line has been scored first. A bone folder is a traditional bookbinder's tool that is best for scoring; score with the pointed end against a ruler. Alternatively, lightly score with a craft knife, breaking the top surface only.

A bone folder is good for folding paper and cardstock too. Press the flat of the bone folder along the fold and run it smoothly along its length. Instead of a bone folder, you can press your thumb along the fold to flatten it.

Strengthening Paper

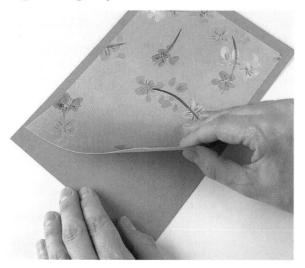

Lightweight paper such as giftwrap can be used to make greeting cards. To strengthen paper, cut a piece of cardstock approximately ⅜ in. (1 cm) larger all around than the finished size (see below left). Spray mount the paper to cardstock, smoothing it outwards from the center. Cut to the required size.

Making an insert

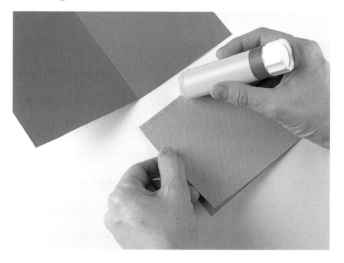

Give a traditional, formal touch to a card by including an insert. It is a useful technique if the cardstock you have chosen for your greeting card is a dark color and difficult to write on clearly; just add an insert in a lighter color. You can also choose a color that contrasts attractively with the cardstock. Open the card out flat. Cut the insert paper at least ¼ in. (5 mm) smaller than the card on all sides. Fold the insert in half. Run a line of paper glue close to the fold of the insert and press it in place inside the card.

Creating a deckle edge

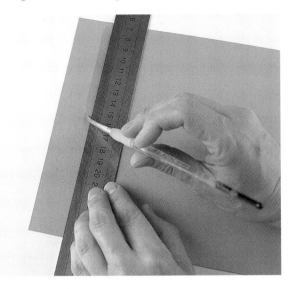

1 Place a ruler on the paper or cardstock where you wish to tear it. Dip an artist's paintbrush in water and run it along the ruler's edge to soften the paper or cardstock. Lightweight paper will not need to be dampened first.

2 Holding the ruler firmly in place, tear the paper against it. For a very irregular edge, tear the paper between your fingers instead. If you want to create a deckle edge on a photo, tear the paper after printing it as the torn edges may get caught in the printer.

Changing the background color of your photographs

Using a computer to change the background color of an image is a good manipulation technique and can completely alter the feel of a photo. It is especially useful when making greeting cards as you can remove any distracting background details and replace them with a solid color.

Always keep the original image untouched and make a copy to work on. Then, if the image is ruined, you have the original to make another copy from. Resize the image to a suitable size following the software instructions.

You can also achieve this technique without the use of a computer. Cut out the image and stick it to another piece of paper with spray adhesive, then photocopy the image.

Cropping photos

Cropping is the term used for cutting away any unnecessary edges from the main subject. On a computer, position the cropping tool on the top left of the image then drag the tool to the bottom right. This will create the outline of a rectangle. Use the mouse to position the four sides of the rectangle to correspond with the points where you intend the new edges to be. Double click the mouse anywhere on the image and the area outside the crop lines will be removed.

However, you may prefer to print the image and manually crop it when making the greeting card. You will have to cut it out anyway and you will have a better idea of what size you wish the finished image to be while creating the card. Place strips of white paper over the edges of the image to judge the size. Lightly mark the position with a pencil, then use a T-square or square ruler to draw accurate corners. Resting on a cutting mat, cut out the photo with a craft knife, cutting against a metal ruler.

Making an envelope

1 To make a template, measure the card front and draw it on scrap paper, adding ¼ in. (5 mm) to each edge. Draw a flap on the upper edge that is half the depth of the front. Draw the back at the lower edge, 1½ in. (4 cm) less than the depth of the front. Draw a 1 in. (2.5 cm) wide tab each side of the front. Draw a curve at each corner – a button or coin is a useful template for drawing the curves.

2 Cut out the template and draw around it on paper or thin cardstock. Score along the edges of the front with a bone folder or lightly with a craft knife. Fold along the scored lines, folding the back over the tabs.

step 1 (see opposite). Cut the front and flap from lining paper, trimming ¼ in. (5 mm) from the outer edges. Using spray adhesive, stick the lining to the inside of the envelope, ¼ in. (5 mm) from the edges. Continue making up the envelope following steps 2 and 3 (see opposite).

3 Open out the back and the flap again. Apply double-sided tape along the side edges of the back, starting 1 in. (2.5 cm) below the upper edge. Peel off the backing tapes and stick the back over the tabs. Tuck the flap inside the back or seal it with double-sided tape.

Making a padded envelope

Present delicate greeting cards in padded envelopes for extra protection. Measure the card front and draw it on scrap paper, adding ⅜ in. (1 cm) to each edge. Draw up the envelope referring to the instructions for Making an envelope. Cut out the envelope. Cut a second front and back from bubble wrap and stick to the inside of the envelope with spray adhesive, with the smooth side of the bubble wrap face up. Fold the back over the front. Apply double-sided tape to the tabs, starting 2¼ in. (5.5 cm) below the upper edges. Peel off the backing tapes and stick the tabs over the back. Seal the flap with double-sided tape.

Making a lined envelope

Use lightweight paper or giftwrap for the lining so the envelope folds neatly and is not too bulky. Follow the instructions for Making an envelope,

3D New Home

Welcome family or friends to a new home with this contemporary greeting card. The three-dimensional effect is achieved by layering copies of the photo between adhesive foam pads.

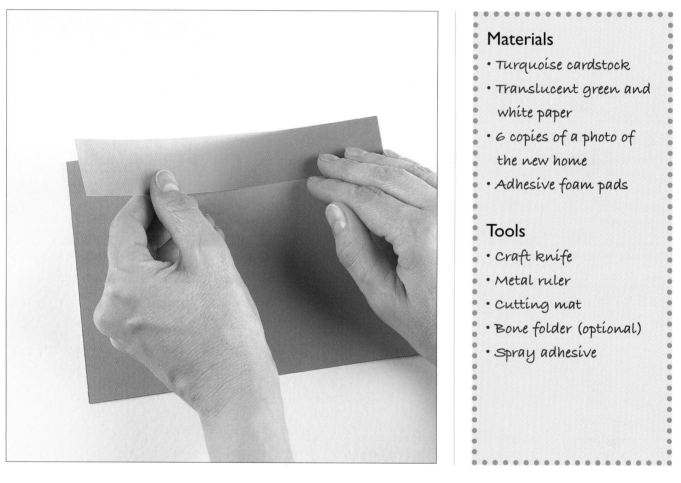

Materials
- Turquoise cardstock
- Translucent green and white paper
- 6 copies of a photo of the new home
- Adhesive foam pads

Tools
- Craft knife
- Metal ruler
- Cutting mat
- Bone folder (optional)
- Spray adhesive

1 Cut an 11½ x 7 in. (27 x 18 cm) rectangle of turquoise cardstock. Using a bone folder or craft knife, score across the center of the cardstock parallel with the short edges. Fold the card in half. Resting on a cutting mat, cut a 7 x 1 in. (18 x 2.5 cm) strip of translucent green paper with a craft knife, cutting the edges against a metal ruler. Adhere the strip across the top edge of the front of the card with spray adhesive.

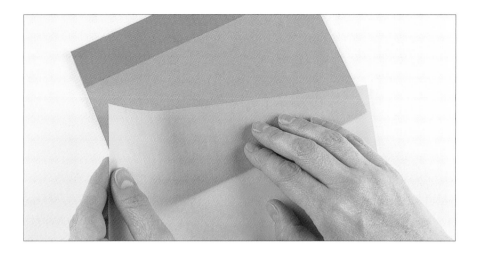

2 Resting on a cutting mat, cut an 8 x 4 in. (20 x 10 cm) rectangle of translucent green paper using a craft knife and a metal ruler. Glue the paper at an angle across the lower section of the card front with spray adhesive.

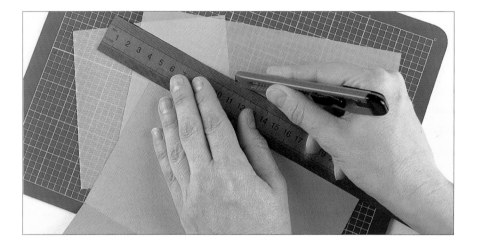

3 Resting on a cutting mat, cut a 4¾ in. (12 cm) square of translucent white paper with a craft knife, cutting against a metal ruler. Glue the paper at an angle across the left-hand edge of the card front with spray adhesive. Turn the card over and trim the excess papers level with the edges of the card.

4 Resting on a cutting mat, cut out the home from one of the copies using a craft knife. Glue the photo off center on the front of the card using spray adhesive.

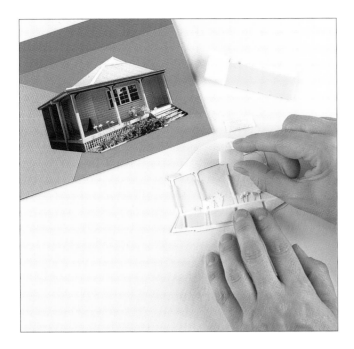

5 Cut out another copy of the home, this time omitting the distant areas, for example, the wall with the window and door and the top of the roof. Stick foam adhesive pads to the back of the photo, cutting them to fit.

6 Peel off the backing papers and carefully place the photo on top of the first copy.

Helpful Hint
Before cutting the rectangle for the greeting card, roughly cut out one photo of the new home to see if the size of the greeting card is suitable; if not, cut the rectangle to a relevant size.

7 Continue cutting out the home, each time discarding more and more of the background areas. Build up the picture by adhering each copy in place with adhesive foam pads.

Valentine Roses

Send a romantic, heartfelt message with this vase of hearts and roses, which are attached on wires so that they can be arranged to stand out from the card.

Materials
- Red and pearlescent turquoise cardstock
- Light pink paper
- Deep pink mesh giftwrap
- Pink relief paint
- Glossy red adhesive-backed acetate
- Photo of red roses
- 22-gauge turquoise wire
- Adhesive foam pads

Tools
- Spray adhesive
- Craft knife
- Metal ruler
- Cutting mat
- Bone folder (optional)
- Tracing paper
- Soft pencil
- Masking tape
- Wire snippers
- Clear sticky tape

1 Glue red cardstock and light pink paper together with spray adhesive then cut a 7⅞ x 7⅛ in. (20 x 18 cm) rectangle. Using a bone folder or craft knife, score across the center of the card parallel with the short edges. Fold the card in half then open it out flat again.

2 Trace the card front, vase and heart template on page 90 onto tracing paper with a pencil. Tape the card front tracing face down on the wrong side of one half of the opened card. Transfer the scallops. Resting on a cutting mat, cut the scallops with a craft knife.

3 Refold the card. Refer to the template to adhere a piece of deep pink mesh giftwrap across the card front with spray adhesive. Trim the excess mesh level with the straight edges of the card front. Open the card out flat to trim around the scallop.

4 Tape the vase tracing face down on the wrong side of a piece of turquoise cardstock. Transfer the vase then cut it out with a craft knife, resting on a cutting mat. Apply spots to the vase with pink relief paint. Set the vase aside to dry.

Helpful Hint

If you do not have wire snippers, use an old pair of scissors to snip the wire. Wire will dull the blades of a new pair.

5 Adhere a 2⅜ in. (6 cm) square of glossy red adhesive-backed acetate to red cardstock. Tape the heart tracing face down on the wrong side with masking tape. Transfer the heart four times.

6 Roughly cut out two photos of red roses. Adhere the roses to red cardstock with spray adhesive. Cut out the roses and hearts with a craft knife, resting on a cutting mat.

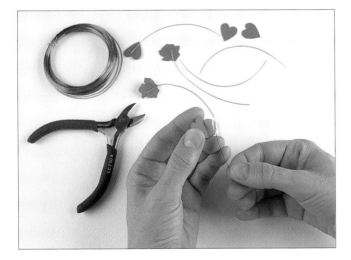

7 Snip turquoise wire into six 4 in. (10 cm) lengths with wire snippers. Secure each length to the back of the roses and hearts with clear sticky tape. Twist the wires on the roses together a few times.

8 Glue foam adhesive pads to the back of the vase, cutting the pads to fit. Peel off the backing tapes and adhere the wires of the roses and hearts to the pads. Check the arrangement by holding the vase against the card front. Adjust the position of the wires if necessary. Snip the wires so they do not extend below the vase. Attach the vase to the card front.

Mother's Day Garden

Paper punches are easy to use and give a professional finish to handmade greeting cards. Flower punches have been used here to echo the flowers in a beautiful garden, making this an ideal card for Mother's day.

Materials
- White cardstock
- Lightweight white Japanese paper
- Horizontal photo of a garden
- Yellow, jade green and lime green paper

Tools
- Spray adhesive
- Craft knife
- Metal ruler
- Cutting mat
- Bone folder (optional)
- Tulip paper punch
- Round flower paper punch
- Decorative-edged scissors
- Thick needle

1 Adhere white cardstock and lightweight white Japanese paper together with spray adhesive, then cut an 11½ x 7 in. (29 x 17.5 cm) rectangle. Using a bone folder or craft knife, score across the center of the card parallel with the short edges. Fold the card in half.

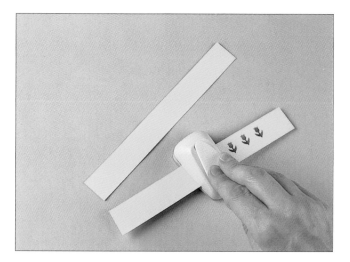

2 Cut the photo to a 5¾ x 3¾ in. (14.5 x 9.5 cm) rectangle. Use spray adhesive to glue the photo to the card front ⅝ in. (1.5 cm) inside the side and upper edges.

3 Cut two 6¼ x 1 in. (16 x 2.5 cm) wide strips of yellow paper. Punch a row of tulips along the strips with a paper punch.

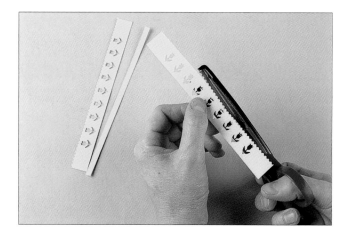

4 Trim the long edges of the strips to ⅛ in. (3 mm) on each side of the tulips, cutting a straight edge on one side and a decorative edge on the other.

5 Use spray adhesive to secure the strips across the photo parallel with the side edges. Cut the ends of the strips level with the upper and lower edges of the card front.

Helpful Hint

To stop small paper items blowing away when applying spray adhesive, lightly spray the surface they are resting on with spray adhesive first.

6 Use a round flower paper punch to punch five flowers from yellow, jade green and lime green paper. Make a hole in the center of the flowers with a thick needle. Use spray adhesive to stick the flowers to the front of the card, overlapping the petals.

7 Punch another five flowers from the colored papers. Make holes in the centers. Stick the flowers inside the card with spray adhesive.

VARIATION

This photo of a happy toddler in a daisy meadow has been cut out with a pair of decorative-edged scissors and then applied to a white card covered with fine, yellow handmade paper. A length of daisy-shaped edging lace is then glued across the photo. A few flowers cut from daisy-shaped edging lace are glued under the photo.

Birthday Truck

Put a budding young truck driver behind the wheels of a smart new vehicle to celebrate their birthday. Add a shiny birthday number to the wagon and attach the wheels with metal paper fasteners so that they will turn.

Materials
- Blue and yellow cardstock
- Gray, purple, yellow, metallic green, red and silver paper
- White acrylic paint
- 2 gold star stickers
- 2 metal paper fasteners
- Photo of child (the head should be approximately ¾ in. (2 cm) wide)

Tools
- Craft knife
- Metal ruler
- Cutting mat
- Bone folder (optional)
- Old ceramic tile or plate
- Flat paintbrush
- Natural sponge
- Spray adhesive
- Tracing paper
- Soft pencil
- Masking tape
- Pencil and compass

1 Cut a 14 x 9 in. (36 x 23 cm) rectangle of light blue cardstock. Using a bone folder or craft knife, score across the center of the card parallel with the short edges. Fold the card in half. Apply a thin coat of white acrylic paint to a ceramic tile or plate with a flat paintbrush. Dab at the paint with a moistened natural sponge then dab the paint onto the top half of the card front in two spots to suggest clouds.

2 Resting on a cutting mat, cut a 9 x ¾ in. (23 x 2 cm) strip of gray paper for the road using a craft knife and cutting against a metal ruler. Glue the road along the lower edge of the front of the card with spray adhesive.

3 Trace the cab, headlamp and relevant number template on pages 90–91 onto tracing paper with a pencil. Tape the cab tracing face down on the wrong side of a piece of purple paper, the headlamp face down on the wrong side of a piece of yellow paper and the number tracing face down on the wrong side of a piece of metallic green paper with masking tape. Transfer the motifs. Resting on a cutting mat, cut out the pieces with a craft knife.

4 Cut out the child from the photo. From red paper, cut a 4⅜ x 3¾ in. (11 x 9.5 cm) rectangle for the wagon. Arrange the cab and wagon on the card front ¾ in. (2 cm) above the road. Slip the child inside the cab. Adhere the pieces in place with spray adhesive. Glue the number on the wagon and apply a gold star sticker on each side.

Helpful Hint
Remember that when adhering pieces with spray adhesive, you have time to reposition them before the adhesive dries.

5 Using the compass, draw two 1½ in. (4 cm) diameter circles onto yellow cardstock for the wheels and two ¾ in. (2 cm) diameter circles onto silver paper for the hubcaps. Resting on a cutting mat, cut out the circles with a craft knife. Attach the hubcaps to the wheels with spray adhesive.

6 Open the greeting card. Resting on a cutting mat, place the wheels in position on the road. Use the point of the compass to make a hole through the center of the wheels and through the card front. Insert the prongs of the paper fasteners through the wheels and the card front. Splay open the prongs on the underside of the card front.

VARIATION

This dashing chap is driving a racy sports car. The door of the car is drawn with a black pen and the fold-down roof is made of fabric. The card has a background of clouds. The template for this card is on page 90.

Father's Day Shirt

Give Dad a card to treasure with this smart shirt complete with a photo of his child tucked into the pocket. The stripes are drawn with a felt pen and the shirt even has real buttons!

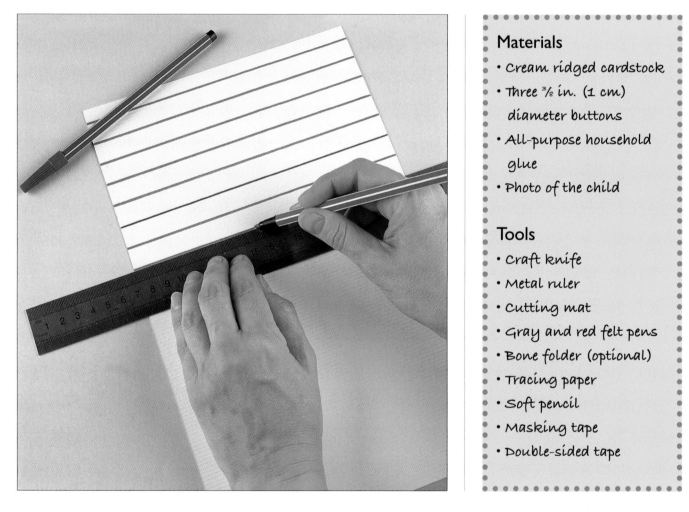

Materials
- Cream ridged cardstock
- Three ⅜ in. (1 cm) diameter buttons
- All-purpose household glue
- Photo of the child

Tools
- Craft knife
- Metal ruler
- Cutting mat
- Gray and red felt pens
- Bone folder (optional)
- Tracing paper
- Soft pencil
- Masking tape
- Double-sided tape

1 Cut a 12 x 7½ in. (30 x 19 cm) rectangle of cream ridged cardstock with the ridges parallel with the short edges. Use a gray felt pen and ruler to draw a line across the card 3⅜ in. (8.5 cm) in from the right-hand edge. Draw lines across the card parallel with the gray line ⅝ in. (1.5 cm) apart using a red felt pen for the shirt stripes.

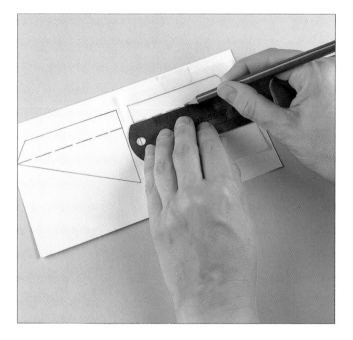

2 Using a bone folder or craft knife, score across the center of the card parallel with the short edges. Fold the card in half then open it out flat again. Refer to the diagram on page 91 to draw the neckline on the front of the card. Resting on a cutting mat, cut along the neckline with a craft knife.

3 Trace the collar template on page 91 onto tracing paper with a pencil. Tape the tracing face down on the wrong side of a piece of cream ridged cardstock. Transfer the collar. Remove the tracing, turn it over and repeat to draw a symmetrical collar. Resting on a cutting mat, cut out the collars with a craft knife.

Helpful Hint
Choose buttons in a color to match the coloring of the photo.

4 Using a bone folder or craft knife, score the collars along the broken lines. Fold back the tabs with the wrong sides facing. Apply double-sided tape to the tabs on the wrong side. Peel off the backing tapes. Slip the collars over the neckline with the collars on the front of the card. Press the tabs to the underside of the front.

5 Refold the card in half along the scored line. Glue the buttons 1⅜ in. (3.5 cm) apart along the center of the front.

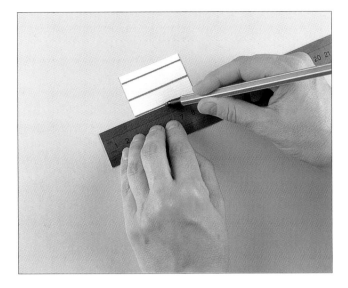

6 Cut a 2⅜ x 2⅛ in. (6 x 5.5 cm) rectangle of cream ridged cardstock, with the ridges parallel with the short edges, for the pocket. Draw lines across the pocket parallel with the short edges ⅝ in. (1.5 cm) apart, using a red felt pen.

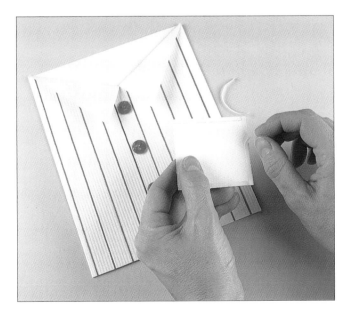

7 Cut ⅛ in. (3 mm) wide strips of double-sided tape. Apply the strips to the long sides and one short side. Peel off the backing tapes. Stick the pocket to the shirt front on the left-hand side.

8 Cut the photo to 1¾ in. (4.5 cm) wide and 2⅜ in. (6 cm) high. Slip the photo into the pocket.

Sequined Thank-You Card

This beautiful card is bordered with a flamboyant ribbon richly beaded with sequins echoing the colors on the photo of a wedding cake. This would be a lovely card to send as a special thank you after a wedding.

1 Cut a 19⅞ x 7½ in. (50.5 x 19 cm) rectangle of pale pink pearlescent cardstock. Using a bone folder or craft knife, score across the cardstock parallel with the short edges, 6⅝ in. (17 cm) and 13¼ in. (34 cm) from the left-hand edge. Fold the card along the scored lines. The left-hand section will be the back and the middle section will be the card front.

Materials
- Pale pink pearlescent cardstock
- Cake photo 5½ x 3½ in. (14 x 9.5 cm)
- Smaller cake photo
- Crystal glitter paint
- 10 in. (25 cm) of 1 in. (2.5 cm) wide pink ribbon
- Flower- and scythe-shaped sequins in pinks and creams
- Tiny pink rocaille beads
- Sewing thread
- Deep cream paper

Tools
- Craft knife
- Metal ruler
- Cutting mat
- Bone folder (optional)
- Spray adhesive
- Medium artist's paintbrush
- Crewel embroidery needle
- Double-sided tape
- Paper glue

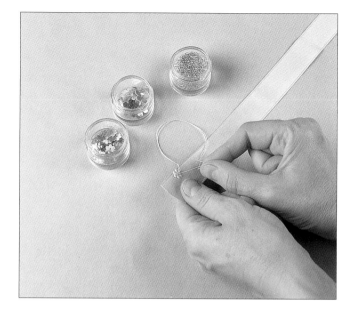

2 Open the card out flat again. Cut the photo to a 5½ x 3½ in. (14 x 9.5 cm) rectangle. Glue the photo to the middle section (the card front) with spray adhesive ⅝ in. (1.5 cm) inside the upper and right-hand edges. Outline the photo with crystal glitter paint. Set aside to dry.

3 To make the sequined ribbon, thread a needle with a double length of sewing thread and knot the ends together. Bring the needle to the right side of the ribbon ⅝ in. (1.5 cm) below one end. Thread on a sequin then a rocaille bead. Insert the needle back through the sequin and pull the thread so the bead sits on the sequin.

4 Continue sewing sequins to the ribbon until 7½ in. (19 cm) of the ribbon is covered. To give some sequins height, thread on one, two or three rocaille beads then one or two sequins and a rocaille bead. Insert the needle back through all the sequins and beads except the last one added. Catch in a few scythe-shaped sequins too.

Helpful Hint
To create an instant card, decorate the card with a ready-made beaded trim.

5 Cut the end of the ribbon to ⅝ in. (1.5 cm) below the sequined section. Turn the ends of the ribbon to the wrong side and secure with double-sided tape. Secure the ribbon ⅝ in. (1.5 cm) inside the left-hand edge.

6 Sew a few sequins to the top right-hand corner of the photo to match the border.

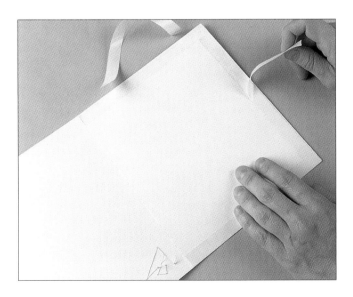

7 Apply double-sided tape to the edges of the right-hand section of the card on the wrong side. Peel off the backing tapes, fold it under the front, and press in place.

8 Cut a 6⅜ x 7 in. (33 x 18 cm) rectangle of deep cream paper for the insert. Fold in half parallel with the short edges. Run a line of paper glue along the fold of the insert and stick it inside the card. Cut out a small photo of a cake and adhere it inside the insert with spray adhesive.

Beaded Celebration Card

A photo of a group of happy friends is embellished with little beads threaded onto colored wire. Choose beads and wire in colors to match the photo.

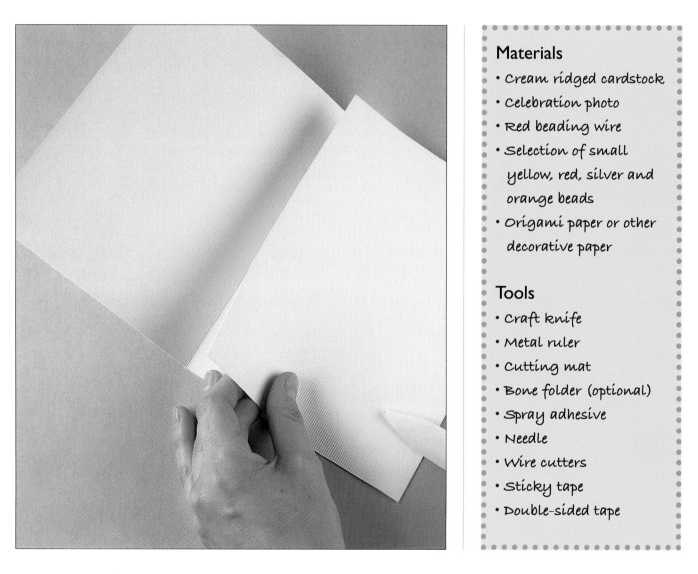

Materials
- Cream ridged cardstock
- Celebration photo
- Red beading wire
- Selection of small yellow, red, silver and orange beads
- Origami paper or other decorative paper

Tools
- Craft knife
- Metal ruler
- Cutting mat
- Bone folder (optional)
- Spray adhesive
- Needle
- Wire cutters
- Sticky tape
- Double-sided tape

1 Cut a 16¾ x 7½ in. (43 x 19 cm) rectangle of cream ridged cardstock. With a bone folder or craft knife, score across the cardstock parallel with the short edges, 5¾ in. (14.5 cm) and 11¼ in. (29 cm) from the left-hand edge. Fold along the scored lines. The left-hand section will be the back and the middle section will be the front.

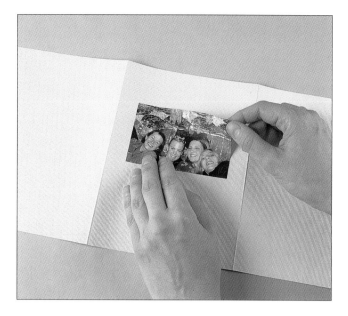

2 Open the card out flat again. Cut the photo to a 4 x 2½ in. (10.5 x 6.5 cm) rectangle. Glue the photo to the card front with spray adhesive 1½ in. (4 cm) below the upper edge and ¾ in. (2 cm) inside the side edges.

3 Pierce a hole with a needle within the top left corner of the photo. Insert a length of wire through the hole and attach the end to the wrong side of the card front with sticky tape.

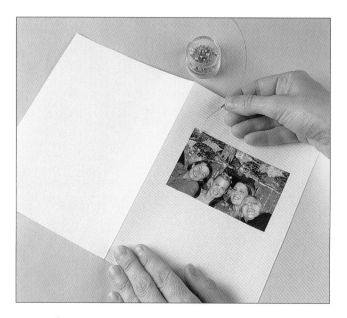

4 Thread a few beads onto the wire on the right side. Pierce a hole ¾ in. (2 cm) above the photo and insert the wire through it.

5 Pierce a hole on the photo beside the first hole and bring the wire through it to the right side. Thread on a few beads and make a stitch. Make another beaded stitch beside it. Tape the end of the wire to the wrong side of the front.

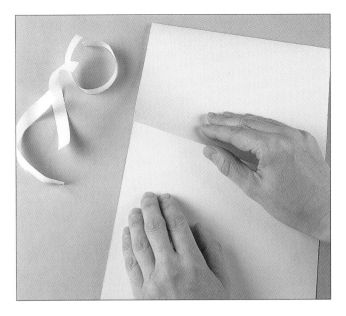

6 Make three beaded stitches with the wire on the lower edge of the photo. Make three rows of beaded stitches horizontally across the card front below the photo, taping the ends of the wire to the wrong side of the card front.

7 Apply double-sided tape to the edges of the right-hand section of the card on the wrong side. Peel off the backing tapes, fold the section under the front and press in place to hide the wire ends.

8 Cut a 7½ x 2¼ in. (19 x 6 cm) strip of origami paper. Tear one edge against a ruler to make the strip ⅝ in. (1.5 cm) wide. Adhere the strip inside the card on the back opening edge with spray adhesive.

Helpful Hint

Make a three-fold card such as this when you need to hide any fixings such as the wire ends. The right-hand section of the card is glued neatly under the card front.

3D Specs

Show off your favorite vacation snaps on the lenses of this wacky pair of sunglasses. Make the specs in a vibrant color and add some gemstones for a showbiz style.

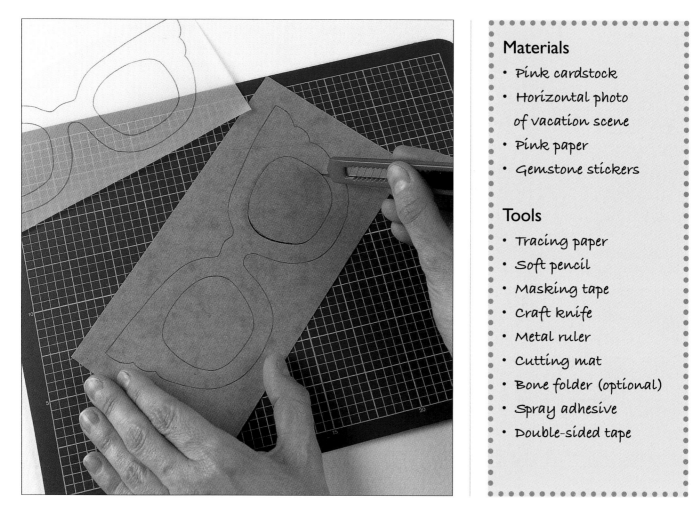

Materials
- Pink cardstock
- Horizontal photo of vacation scene
- Pink paper
- Gemstone stickers

Tools
- Tracing paper
- Soft pencil
- Masking tape
- Craft knife
- Metal ruler
- Cutting mat
- Bone folder (optional)
- Spray adhesive
- Double-sided tape

1 Trace the sunglasses and earpiece templates on page 91 onto tracing paper with a pencil. Tape the sunglasses face down on the right side of a piece of pink cardstock with masking tape. Transfer the sunglasses. Remove the tracing. Resting on a cutting mat, cut out the windows with a craft knife.

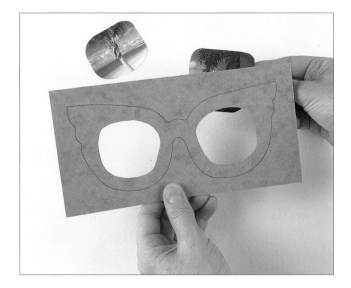

2 Resting on a cutting mat, use a craft knife to cut out two images from the photo about ¼ in. (5 mm) larger all around than the windows. Spray the wrong side of the sunglasses with spray adhesive and position the images behind the windows.

3 Adhere the sunglasses to a piece of pink paper with spray adhesive. Resting on a cutting mat, cut out the sunglasses with a craft knife.

4 Tape the earpiece tracing face down on the wrong side of a piece of pink cardstock. Transfer the earpiece. Remove the tracing, turn it over and repeat to draw a symmetrical earpiece. Resting on a cutting mat, cut out the pieces with a craft knife.

Helpful Hint
If using cardstock that is colored on one side only, color the other side of the earpieces with same-colored paper attached with spray adhesive.

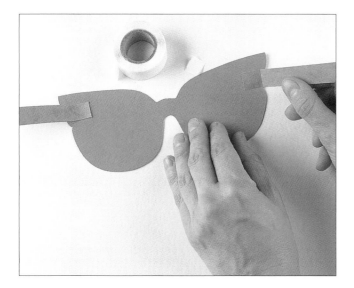

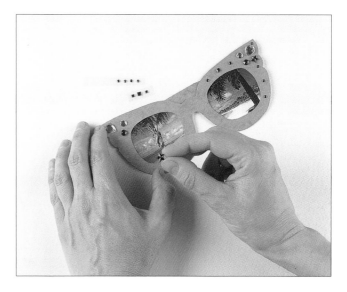

5 Using a bone folder or craft knife, score the earpieces along the broken lines. Fold back the tabs with the wrong sides facing. Apply double-sided tape to the tabs on the right side. Peel off the backing tapes and attach the tabs to the back of the sunglasses.

6 Decorate the edges of the sunglasses by sticking on gemstone stickers.

VARIATION

Black and white city images work well on the sunglasses too. This pair is made of turquoise pearlescent cardstock with stripes painted with purple glitter paint. Apply the glitter paint before glueing the photos in place to avoid getting glitter on them.

Filmstrip Bookmark

Create a realistic filmstrip of favorite photos such as these classic vacation shots. The greeting card is a gift too, as the strip can be removed to use as a bookmark.

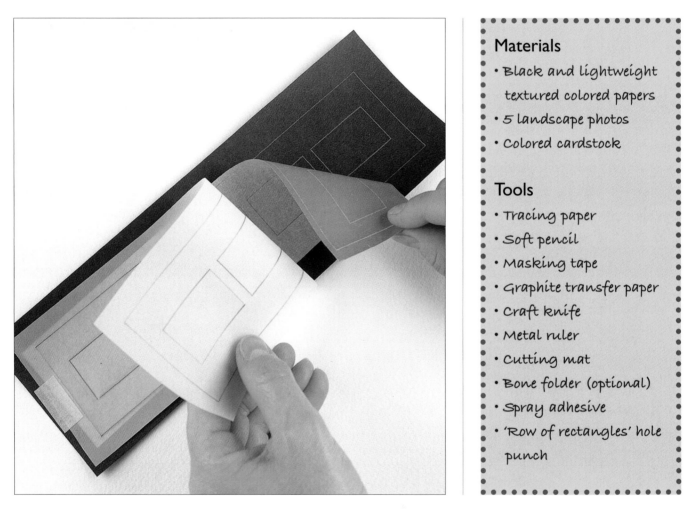

Materials
- Black and lightweight textured colored papers
- 5 landscape photos
- Colored cardstock

Tools
- Tracing paper
- Soft pencil
- Masking tape
- Graphite transfer paper
- Craft knife
- Metal ruler
- Cutting mat
- Bone folder (optional)
- Spray adhesive
- 'Row of rectangles' hole punch

1 Trace the bookmark and card front template on page 92 onto tracing paper. Tape the bookmark tracing face down on the wrong side of a piece of black paper. Slip a piece of graphite transfer paper underneath, graphite side down. Redraw the image to transfer the bookmark. Resting on a cutting mat, cut out the bookmark and windows with a craft knife.

2 Cut the photos to 1⅝ x 1¼ in. (4 x 3 cm), cutting the long edges parallel with the lower edge. Spray the wrong side of the bookmark with spray adhesive. Adhere the photos behind the windows, checking as you go to make sure they are correctly positioned.

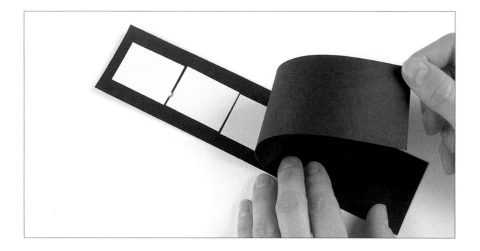

3 Cut a strip of black paper 8⅝ x 2 in. (22 x 5 cm). Spray one side with spray adhesive and adhere the strip to the back of the bookmark.

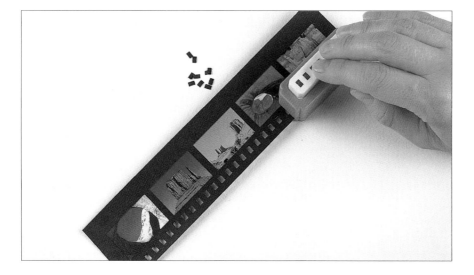

4 Using a hole puncher and working outwards from the center, punch a row of rectangles along the long edges of the bookmark.

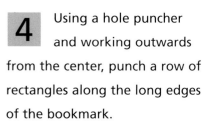

5 Take a piece of colored cardstock and some lightweight textured paper and glue them together with spray adhesive. Cut a 9⅞ x 6¼ in. (25 x 16 cm) rectangle for the greeting card. Using a bone folder or craft knife, score across the center of the card parallel with the long edge. Fold the card in half then open it out flat again.

6 Tape the card front tracing face down on the wrong side of one half of the opened card with masking tape. Transfer the slits. Resting on a cutting mat, cut the slits with a craft knife. Punch a row of rectangles at the top of the left-hand edge and the bottom of the right-hand edge of the card front. Insert the bookmark through the slits.

Helpful Hint
To make this greeting card look really professional, choose your lightweight paper and cardstock in a color to coordinate with the photos.

Bobble-head Pet

The expressive head of this appealing dog can be manipulated to create different poses. It will also nod comically because the head is attached on a wire spring.

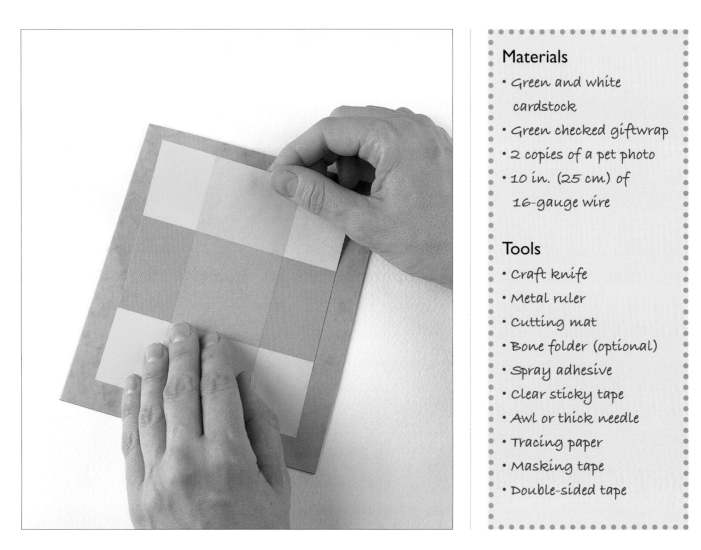

Materials
- Green and white cardstock
- Green checked giftwrap
- 2 copies of a pet photo
- 10 in. (25 cm) of 16-gauge wire

Tools
- Craft knife
- Metal ruler
- Cutting mat
- Bone folder (optional)
- Spray adhesive
- Clear sticky tape
- Awl or thick needle
- Tracing paper
- Masking tape
- Double-sided tape

1 Resting on a cutting mat, cut an 11 x 6¼ in. (28 x 16 cm) rectangle of green cardstock. Using a bone folder or craft knife, score across the center of the card parallel with the short edges. Fold the card in half. Cut a 5⅛ x 4¼ in. (13 x 11 cm) rectangle of checked giftwrap. Adhere the giftwrap to the card front with spray adhesive.

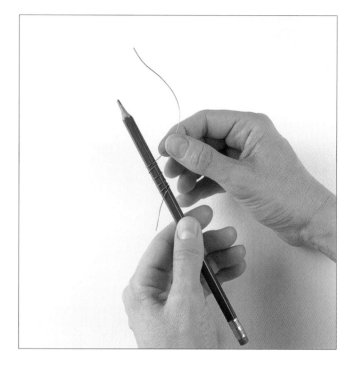

2 Resting on a cutting mat, cut out the pet with a craft knife, cutting away the outer edges of the head. Adhere the pet to the giftwrap rectangle with spray adhesive.

3 To make a wire spring, wrap a 10 in. (25 cm) length of wire around a pencil to coil it. Leave about 1 in. (2.5 cm) at each end uncoiled.

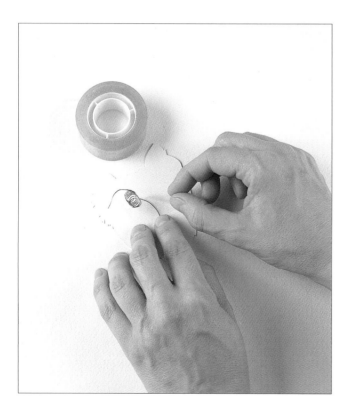

4 Glue another photo of the pet to white cardstock with spray adhesive. Resting on a cutting mat, cut out the head with a craft knife. Attach one end of the wire spring to the back of the head with a piece of clear sticky tape.

Helpful Hint
The ideal thickness of the wire needed to make the spring is 16 gauge. Alternatively, snip a section from the wire spiral of an old spiral bound notebook to use as a spring.

5 Open the card out flat. Place the head in position on the pet. Use an awl or a thick needle to make a hole through the card front under the spring. Insert the end of the spring through the hole.

6 Apply double-sided tape to the wrong side of a 1¾ in. (4 cm) square of giftwrap. Trace the star sticker template on page 92 onto tracing paper with a pencil. Tape the tracing face down on the wrong side of the giftwrap with masking tape. Transfer the star. Remove the tracing. Resting on a cutting mat, cut out the star with a craft knife, cutting against a metal ruler.

7 Peel the backing tapes off the star. Stick the star over the wire on the inside of the greeting card.

Silk Wedding

Use a special paste to transfer a cherished wedding photo to silk to make a beautiful anniversary card. The greeting card is then enhanced with gold stitching and organza ribbon.

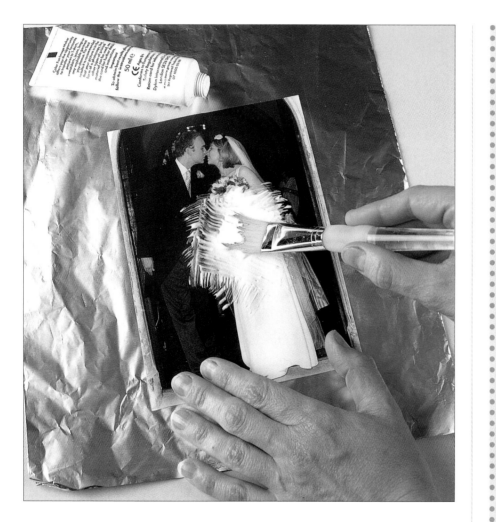

Materials

- Photocopy of photo
  7 x 5 in. (18 x 13 cm)
- 10½ x 8¼ in. (25 x 21 cm)
  white silk douppioni
- White handmade paper
- Gold machine
  embroidery thread
- 24 in. (60 cm) of 1 in.
  (2.5 cm) wide golden
  organza ribbon

Tools

- Baking foil
- Fabric transfer paste
- Old large paintbrush
- Old plastic grocery bag
- Brayer
- Paper towels
- Sponge
- Fabric scissors
- Craft knife
- Metal ruler
- Cutting mat
- Bone folder (optional)
- Double hole punch

1 Place the photo, printed side up, on a piece of baking foil. Squeeze the transfer paste onto the photo. Spread a thick layer of paste over the entire photo with an old large paintbrush. The paste should be thick enough to obscure the image.

2 Cut open a plastic grocery bag and lay it out flat to protect the work surface. Place the silk douppioni on top. Carefully lift the photo by the corners and place it face down on the silk. Smooth the paper outwards from the center. Place a paper towel on top.

3 Lightly run a brayer over the surface to squeeze out the excess paste. Continue rolling the brayer over the surface in all directions, applying more pressure to ensure the entire photo adheres to the silk. Blot up the excess paste with the paper towel. Leave the paste to dry for at least four hours or, ideally, overnight.

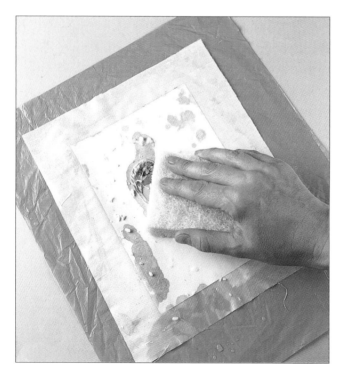

4 Soak a sponge in water. Place the sponge on the photo for a few minutes to soak the paper. Carefully rub away the paper to reveal the image on the silk. Leave to dry. Continue rubbing away the fuzzy remains of the paper with a damp sponge until all the paper is removed. Leave to dry.

Helpful Hint
Moisten the paper with a paintbrush if it is too thick to tear. The water will weaken the paper making it easier to remove.

5 Squeeze a little paste onto the photo and brush it evenly over the entire image to seal it. Leave to dry, ideally overnight as before. Cut out the photo leaving a ¼ in. (5 mm) border all around.

6 To tear a deckle edge, place a ruler on handmade paper. Tear the paper against the ruler to make two 9 x 8¼ in. (23.5 x 21 cm) rectangles. Glue the photo to one rectangle 1 in. (2.5 cm) in from the short top and long right-hand edge with spray adhesive. This will be the card front.

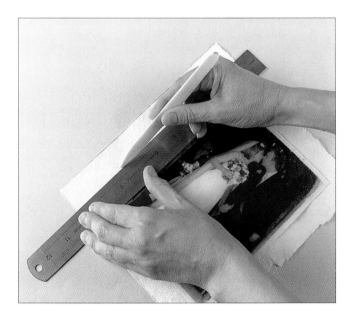

7 Using a bone folder or craft knife, score across the card front 1¼ in. (3 cm) in from the long left-hand edge with a bone folder or craft knife to make a hinge. Bend the hinge forwards.

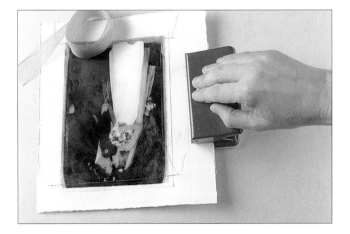

8 Use a sewing machine to stitch across the top and lower edges of the photo with gold machine embroidery thread. Pull the thread ends to the front; knot the ends. Place the front on the back, punch a pair of holes through the hinge with a hole punch. Thread ribbon through the holes and tie into a bow.

Circles of Friends

Use scraps of colored cardstock and papers to encircle photos of a group of friends. The large circles stand out from the card because they are applied with foam adhesive pads.

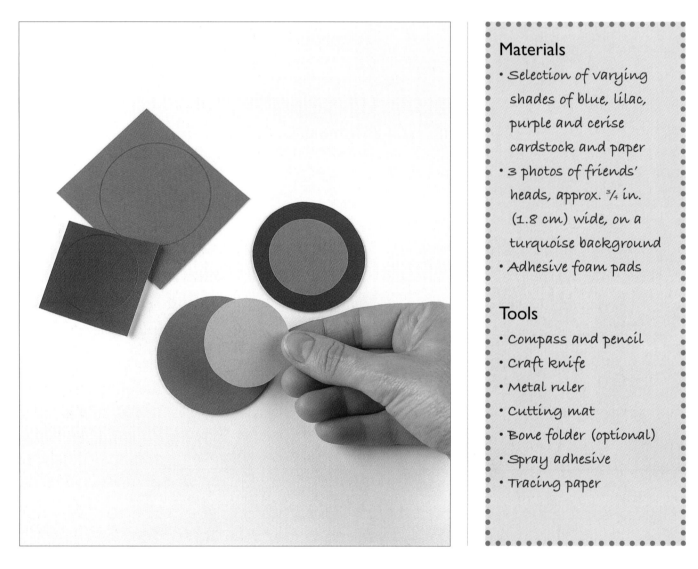

Materials
- Selection of varying shades of blue, lilac, purple and cerise cardstock and paper
- 3 photos of friends' heads, approx. ¾ in. (1.8 cm) wide, on a turquoise background
- Adhesive foam pads

Tools
- Compass and pencil
- Craft knife
- Metal ruler
- Cutting mat
- Bone folder (optional)
- Spray adhesive
- Tracing paper

1 Draw one 2¼ in. (6 cm) diameter circle each on the purple, medium blue and deep blue cardstock. Cut out the circles with a craft knife, resting on a cutting mat. Cut three 1⅝ in. (4 cm) diameter circles of lilac and purple paper. Adhere the paper circles on the card circles with spray adhesive.

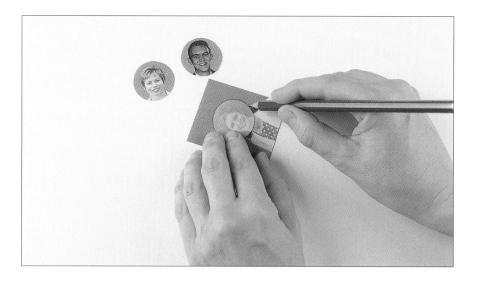

2 Cut out a 1¼ in. (3 cm) diameter circle of tracing paper. Position the tracing on one photo, centering the head. Draw around the circle and cut it out. Repeat on the other heads. Adhere the heads to the paper circles.

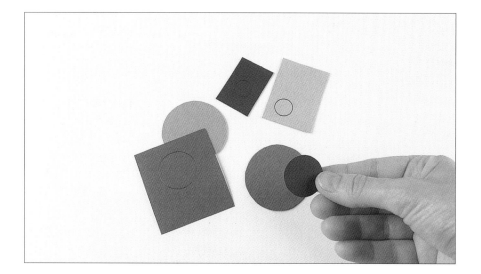

3 Cut out one 1¾ in. (4.5 cm) diameter circle from both cerise and bright blue cardstock. Cut one 1 in. (2.5 cm) diameter circle from both lilac and purple paper and one ⅜ in. (1 cm) diameter circle from both pale blue and deep blue paper. Adhere the paper circles to the card circles with spray adhesive.

4 Cut an 11 x 9 in. (28 x 23 cm) rectangle of lilac cardstock. Using a bone folder or craft knife, score across the center of the card, parallel with the short edges. Fold the card in half.

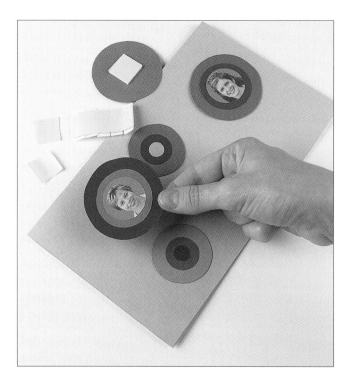

5 Arrange the circles on the card front. Adhere the smaller circles in place with spray adhesive and the large circles with foam adhesive pads.

Helpful Hint
Use a computer to change the background color to turquoise for all the photos. Alternatively, cut them out and attach to turquoise paper, then photocopy them.

VARIATION
This colorful rocking card is created by cutting a circle of cardstock the same size as the outer card circle, folding it in half and sticking it to the back of the lower half of the outer circle. This creates an 'easel'.

New Baby

This understated card is quick to make and features a selection of interesting decorations. It's a great way to use up odd buttons and lace. The gilded paper used here can be found in Chinese supermarkets or you can create your own.

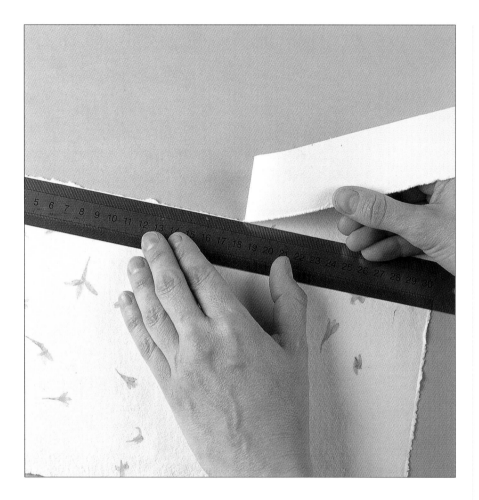

Materials
- Handmade paper embedded with petals
- 8 in. (20 cm) of 1 in. (2.5 cm) wide white edging lace
- Black and white photo of mother and baby
- Sheet of gilded Chinese paper
- 3 mother-of-pearl buttons

Tools
- Metal ruler
- Medium size artist's paintbrush
- Bone folder (optional)
- Spray adhesive
- Scissors
- Craft knife
- Cutting mat
- All-purpose household glue

1 To tear a deckle edge, place a ruler on handmade paper embedded with petals. Moisten a medium artist's paintbrush and run it along the paper against the ruler to weaken the paper. Tear the paper against the ruler to make a 13½ x 6¾ in. (34 x 17 cm) rectangle for the greeting card.

2 Using a bone folder or craft knife, score across the center of the greeting card parallel with the short edges. Fold the card in half.

3 Adhere a length of white edging lace to the greeting card ⅜ in. (1 cm) in from the opening edge with spray adhesive. Cut the ends level with the upper and lower edges of the card.

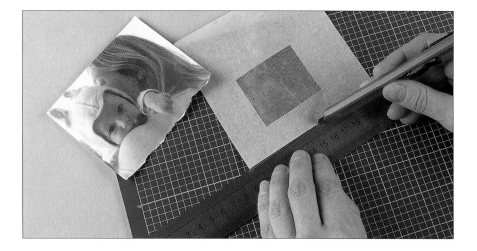

4 Tear across the lower edge of the photo, then cut the other edges with a straight edge to 4 x 3⅛ in. (10 x 8 cm). Cut a ¾ in. (2 cm) wide margin around the gilded rectangle of a sheet of Chinese paper.

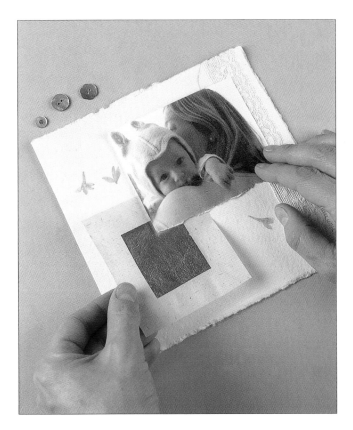

5 Arrange the photo on the card front and slip the gilded rectangle under one corner. Adhere in place with spray adhesive. Glue three buttons to the card front.

Helpful Hint
If Chinese paper is unavailable, paint a rectangle on fine paper with gold paint, or use a piece of gold leaf.

VARIATION

This card with its cheery youngster uses small amounts of unusual textured papers. Rectangles of lightweight Japanese papers are layered on pale blue handmade paper which has been torn with a deckle edge. Narrow edging lace and buttons are then glued to the card. You could add a ready-made adhesive motif such as a teddy or a flower, available at craft suppliers.

Family Tree

This elegant card of a traditional family tree is ideal for many special family occasions and is sure to be treasured by the recipient. The portraits are attached with small silver brads.

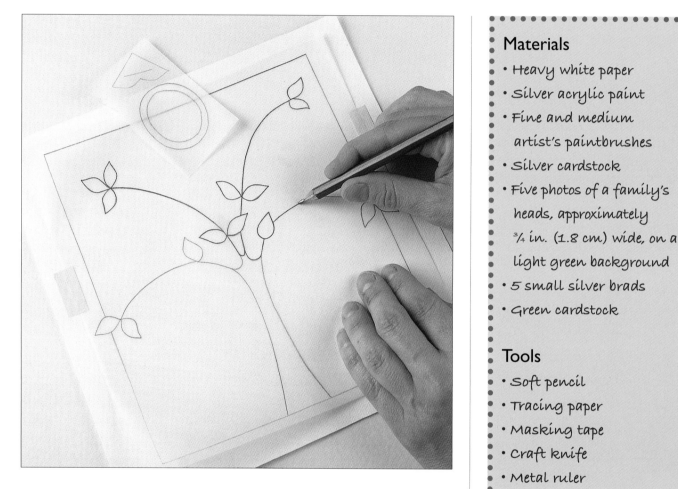

Materials
- Heavy white paper
- Silver acrylic paint
- Fine and medium artist's paintbrushes
- Silver cardstock
- Five photos of a family's heads, approximately ¾ in. (1.8 cm) wide, on a light green background
- 5 small silver brads
- Green cardstock

Tools
- Soft pencil
- Tracing paper
- Masking tape
- Craft knife
- Metal ruler
- Cutting mat
- Bone folder (optional)
- Spray adhesive
- Awl
- All-purpose household glue
- Paper glue

1 Enlarge the tree template on page 93 to 150% on a photocopier and then trace, along with the oval and corner mount templates, onto tracing paper with a pencil. Tape the tree tracing face down on the right side of the heavy white paper with masking tape. Transfer the tree. Remove the tracing.

2 Paint the tree with silver acrylic paint using fine and medium artist's paintbrushes. Leave it to dry. Resting on a cutting mat, use a craft knife to cut out the picture of the tree, cutting around the leaves that fall outside the frame.

3 Tape the large oval tracing face down on the wrong side of a piece of silver cardstock with masking tape. Transfer the oval five times. Remove the tracing. Resting on a cutting mat, use a craft knife to cut out the large ovals.

4 Cut the tracing of the small oval away from the larger one. Position it on one photo, centering the head. Draw around the oval and cut it out. Repeat on the other heads. Adhere the heads to the large ovals with spray adhesive.

5 Resting on a cutting mat, arrange the ovals on the tree. Pierce a hole through the top of the ovals and through the white paper. Insert a brad through the hole on each oval then through the holes in the paper. Splay the prongs open on the underside.

6 Tape the corner mount tracing face down on the wrong side of a piece of silver cardstock. Remove the tracing. Resting on a cutting mat, use a craft knife to cut out the corner mount and slits. Repeat three times. Slip the corners of the picture of the tree through the slits.

7 Cut a 16¼ x 8⅞ in. (41 x 22.5 cm) rectangle of green cardstock. Using a bone folder or craft knife, score across the center of the card parallel with the short edges. Fold the card in half. Center the picture of the tree on the card front. Glue the corner mounts to the card front.

8 Cut a 15 x 7⅝ in. (38 x 19.5 cm) rectangle of heavy white paper for the insert. Fold in half parallel with the short edges. Run a line of paper glue along the fold of the insert and glue it inside the card.

VARIATION

Here is a contemporary version of mounting a family photo on a greeting card. Striped giftwrap is applied to cardstock for the greeting card. Two lengths of colored metal are coiled tightly with a pair of jewelry pliers and slipped onto the top and lower edges of the photo. The coils are then glued to the card front.

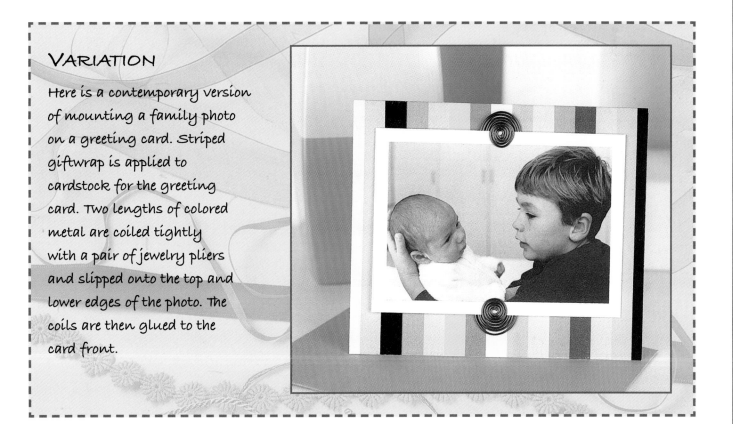

Sporty Birthday Card

Commemorate an active vacation by creating a birthday card that displays lots of cherished moments. This card has a landscape background photo to set the scene with other photos layered on top.

Materials
- White cardstock
- Picture of a sporting scene 7 x 5¼ in. (17.5 x 13.5 cm)
- Red corrugated cardstock
- 2 photos of sporting scenes or friends
- Fawn cardstock
- Fine twine

Tools
- Craft knife
- Metal ruler
- Cutting mat
- Bone folder (optional)
- Spray adhesive
- Soft pencil
- Tracing paper
- Masking tape
- Hole punch
- Awl

1 Cut a 10½ x 7 in. (27 x 17.5 cm) rectangle of white cardstock. Using a bone folder or craft knife, score across the center of the card parallel with the short edges. Fold the card in half. Adhere the landscape photo to the card front with spray adhesive.

2 Cut a 3 in. (7.5 cm) square of red corrugated cardstock. Adhere the square to the top right-hand corner of the card front with spray adhesive. Cut one photo to a 2⅛ in. (5.5 cm) square. Glue the photo ¼ in. (5 mm) inside the lower and right-hand edges with spray adhesive.

3 Cut a 4¾ x 2¾ in. (12 x 7 cm) rectangle of red corrugated cardstock. Adhere the rectangle ⅝ in. (1.5 cm) inside the top and left-hand edges with spray adhesive.

4 Trace the label template on page 93 onto tracing paper with a pencil. Tape the tracing face down on the right side of a piece of fawn cardstock with masking tape. Transfer the label. Remove the tracing. Resting on a cutting mat, cut out the label with a craft knife. Punch a hole at the top with a hole punch.

Helpful Hint
If you do not have colored corrugated cardstock, paint ordinary corrugated cardstock from packaging.

5 Cut the remaining photo to a 2½ x 2 in. (6.5 x 5 cm) square. Glue the photo ¼ in. (5 mm) inside the lower and right-hand edges with spray adhesive.

6 Resting on a cutting mat, pierce a hole with an awl through the card ¼ in. (5 mm) below the fold and 2 in. (5 cm) in from the left-hand edge. Thread a length of fine twine through the hole on the label then the hole on the card. Knot the ends of the twine together so the label hangs in front of the corrugated cardstock rectangle.

Retirement Landscape

Border a tranquil landscape photo with falling leaves. The leaves are quick to create with a rubber stamp, so you can decorate the card as simply or lavishly as you wish.

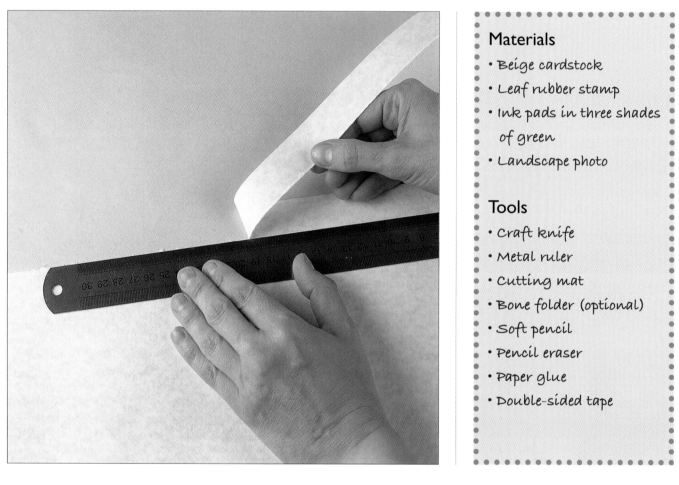

Materials
- Beige cardstock
- Leaf rubber stamp
- Ink pads in three shades of green
- Landscape photo

Tools
- Craft knife
- Metal ruler
- Cutting mat
- Bone folder (optional)
- Soft pencil
- Pencil eraser
- Paper glue
- Double-sided tape

1 Cut a 24¼ x 9 in. (61 x 22.5 cm) rectangle of beige cardstock. To create a deckle edge, tear off 1 in. (2.5 cm) along one long edge using a ruler.

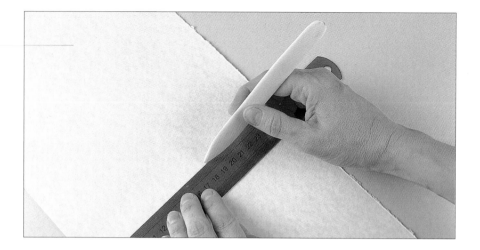

2 Using a bone folder or craft knife, score across the card parallel with the short edges, 8⅛ in. (20.5 cm) and 16¼ in. (41 cm) from the left-hand edge. Fold along the scored lines; the left-hand section will be the back and the middle section will be the card front. Open the card out flat again.

3 Lightly draw a window 5⅜ x 4 in. (13.5 x 10 cm) on the card front 1¼ in. (3 cm) inside the upper and right-hand edge. Use rubber stamps to stamp leaves overlapping the lower and left-hand edge of the window using shades of green ink. Stamp a few leaves on the right-hand edge of the front.

4 Leave the ink to dry then carefully rub away any visible pencil lines on the leaves with a pencil eraser. Resting on a cutting mat and using a craft knife, cut out the window, cutting around the leaves that extend onto the window.

5 Cut the photo to 6⅛ x 4¾ in. (15.5 x 12 cm). Glue the photo under the window with paper glue.

Helpful Hint

If the stamp you are using has two images on it and you only want to stamp one of them, stick a piece of masking tape over the image that isn't required, stamp onto the ink pad then peel off the masking tape. Stamp the image onto the card.

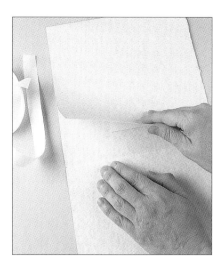

6 Stamp leaves on a piece of beige cardstock using three shades of green ink. Using a craft knife and resting on a cutting mat, cut out the leaves. Glue them around the left-hand and lower edges of the window.

7 Apply double-sided tape to the edges of the right-hand section of the card on the wrong side. Peel off the backing tapes, fold the section under the front and press in place.

8 Stamp a few leaves at random inside the card using three shades of green ink.

VARIATION

A trio of beach huts are stamped onto this colorful greeting card. The roofs of the beach huts butt into the window framing a nautical photo. The seagulls on the left-hand side of the card have also been stamped but if a similar stamp isn't available, draw them on with felt pen.

Christmas Ornaments

Celebrate the festive season with these vibrant Christmas decorations.

If you want to make a series of quick Christmas cards, send single-photo ornaments on cord, ready to hang on the Christmas tree.

Materials
- Photo of Christmas tree
- Light green and pink glittery giftwrap
- Fine blue Japanese paper
- White and pink cardstock
- Gold paper
- Fine gold cord

Tools
- Craft knife
- Metal ruler
- Cutting mat
- Bone folder (optional)
- Spray adhesive
- Soft pencil
- Tracing paper
- Masking tape
- Double-sided tape
- Awl

1 Adhere the photo, a 4 in. (10 cm) square of light green glittery giftwrap and fine blue Japanese paper to white cardstock with spray adhesive.

2 Trace the ornament templates on page 93 onto tracing paper with a pencil. Tape the long ornament tracing face down on the right side of the photo using masking tape. Tape the other ornament tracings face down on the right side of the squares. Transfer the ornaments. Remove the tracings. Resting on a cutting mat, cut out the ornaments with a craft knife.

3 Apply double-sided tape to the wrong side of a piece of gold paper. Tape one ornament tracing face down on the double-sided tape with masking tape. Transfer the ornament hanger three times. Resting on a cutting mat, cut out the hangers with a craft knife. Peel off the backing tapes and stick the hangers to the top of the ornaments.

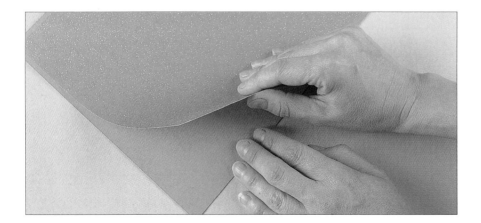

4 Glue pink cardstock and pink glittery giftwrap together with spray adhesive, then cut a 13 x 7½ in. (33 x 19 cm) rectangle for the greeting card. Using a bone folder or craft knife, score across the center of the card parallel with the long edges. Fold the card in half.

5 Resting on a cutting mat, use an awl to pierce three evenly-spaced holes through the card ¼ in. (5 mm) below the fold and 1¾ in. (4.5 cm) in from the side edges. Thread a length of fine gold cord through the hole on one ornament and knot the end on the underside. Thread the cord through the hole on the card. Knot the end on the back of the card. Repeat on the other ornaments so they hang at different levels.

Helpful Hint

Dab the ends of fine cord with glue to stop them unravelling.

VARIATION

This Christmas puzzle card is quick and easy to make. A photo is glued to colored cardstock with spray adhesive. A festive message is written on the back, then the photo is cut into squares to be pieced together by the recipient to reveal the Christmas picture and message.

Christmas Fairy

This cute fairy is embellished with sparkling sequins, glitter and gemstones. Her outfit is highlighted with sequin dust and the photo is applied to cardstock covered with Japanese paper and bordered with organza fabric.

1 Take your photograph and mark out a 4 in. (10 cm) square. To create a deckle edge, tear the edges of the photo against a ruler.

Materials
- Black and white photo of child dressed as fairy
- 5 large silver sequins
- 2 pink cabochons
- Selection of small pink star-shaped sequins
- Gold and crystal relief glitter paints
- Medium paintbrush
- Gold and crystal sequin dust
- Lightweight cream Japanese paper
- Cream cardstock
- Scrap of pink organza

Tools
- Metal ruler
- All-purpose household glue
- Craft knife
- Cutting mat
- Bone folder (optional)
- Spray adhesive
- Fabric scissors

Helpful Hint
Use colored tissue or translucent paper instead of organza fabric if you prefer.

2 Glue a large silver sequin to the center of the headdress and end of the wand. Glue a pink cabochon on the center of the sequins.

3 Apply gold relief glitter paint to the headdress, areas of the fairy's outfit such as the belt, and along the wand. Sprinkle gold sequin dust on the headdress and wand; shake off the excess.

4 Paint a thin coat of crystal relief glitter paint on the wings with a medium paintbrush. Sprinkle gold sequin dust and small pink star-shaped sequins around the edges. Shake off the excess and nudge the particles into place with the tip of a paintbrush. Leave to dry. Dab gold relief glitter paint onto the background, sprinkle crystal sequin dust on top then shake off the excess. Leave to dry.

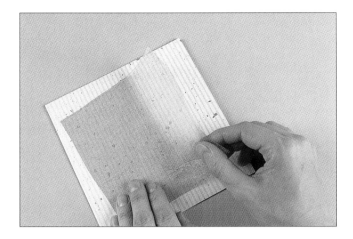

5 Stick cream cardstock and lightweight cream Japanese paper together with spray adhesive then cut a rectangle 12 x 6 in. (30 x 15 cm). Using a bone folder or craft knife, score across the center of the card parallel with the short edges. Fold the card in half. Roughly cut a 4¾ in. (12 cm) square of pink organza fabric with fabric scissors. Secure at an angle on the card front using spray adhesive.

6 Center the photo on top and adhere with spray adhesive. Glue a few sequins in clusters on the edges of the photo.

VARIATION

You can use this same technique to make a rectangle card using a similar image.

Alternatively, make this fun Halloween card. The photo of the scary characters is applied to pink cardstock covered with Japanese paper and a piece of purple paper set at a jaunty angle.

Templates

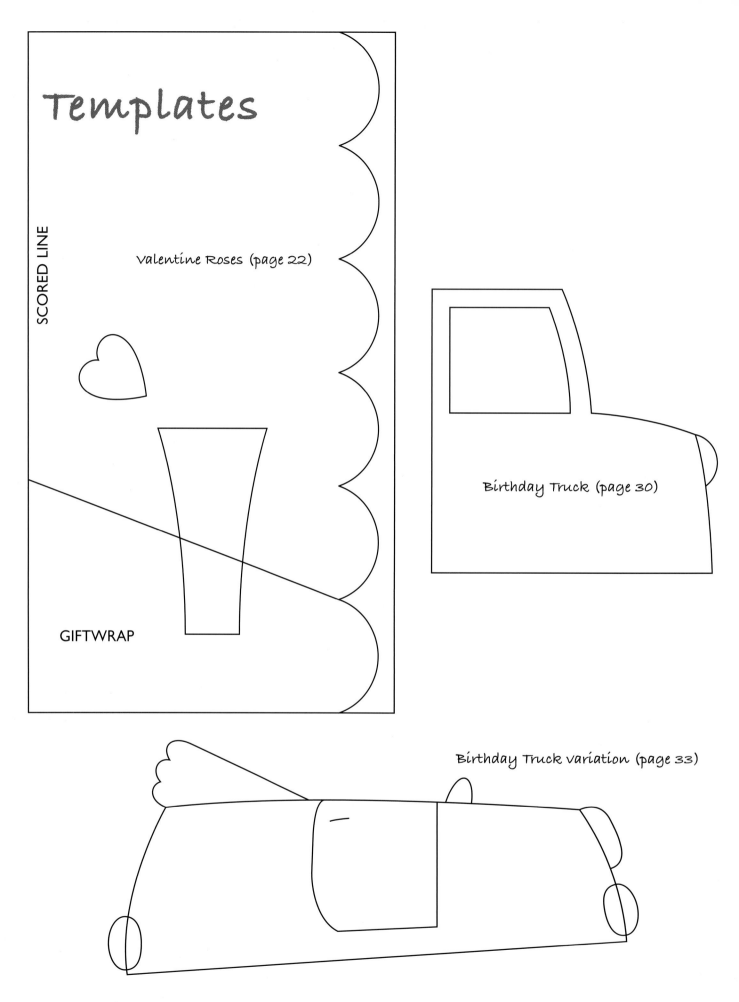

SCORED LINE

Valentine Roses (page 22)

GIFTWRAP

Birthday Truck (page 30)

Birthday Truck variation (page 33)

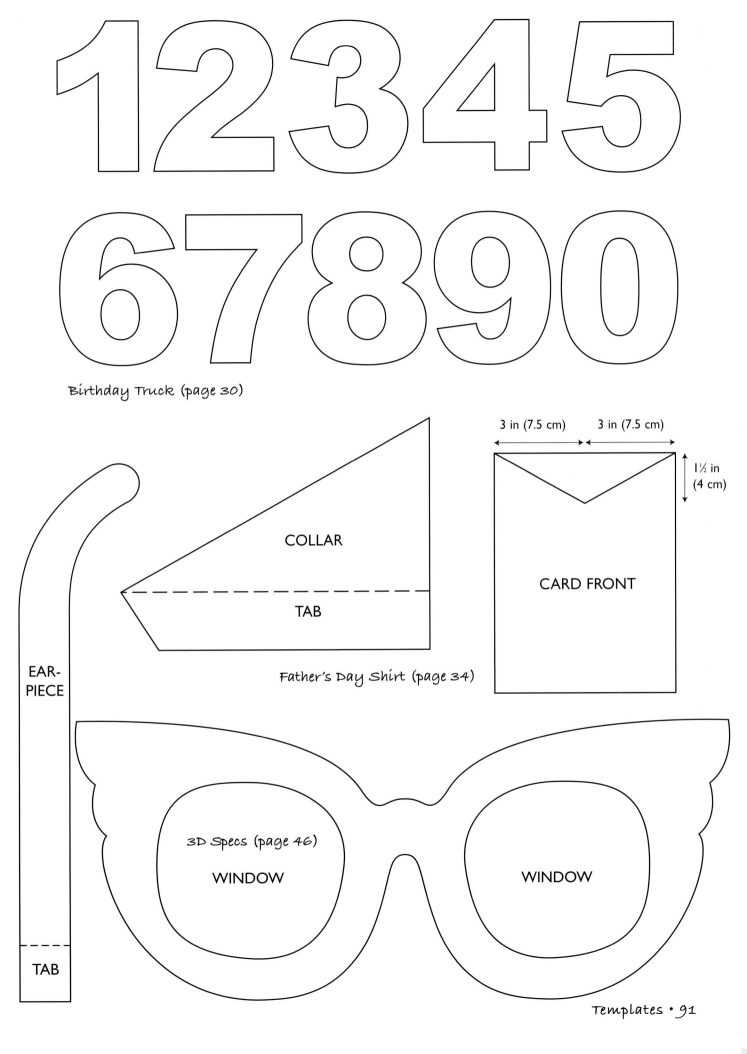

1 2 3 4 5
6 7 8 9 0

Birthday Truck (page 30)

COLLAR

TAB

Father's Day Shirt (page 34)

3 in (7.5 cm)   3 in (7.5 cm)

1½ in (4 cm)

CARD FRONT

EAR-
PIECE

TAB

3D Specs (page 46)

WINDOW

WINDOW

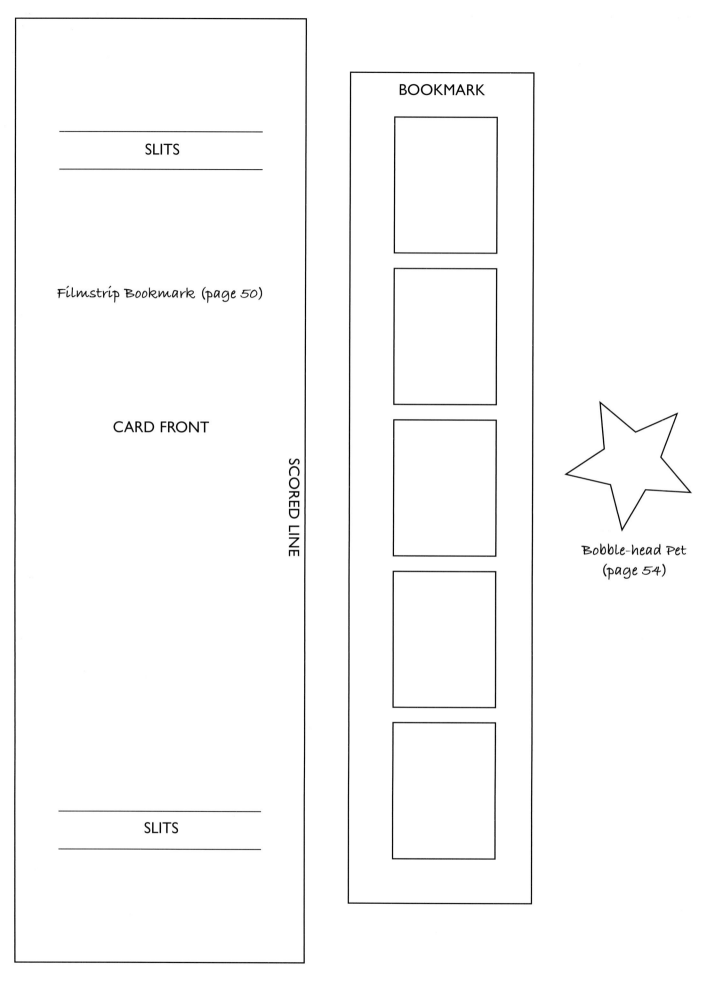

SLITS

Filmstrip Bookmark (page 50)

CARD FRONT

SCORED LINE

SLITS

BOOKMARK

Bobble-head Pet
(page 54)

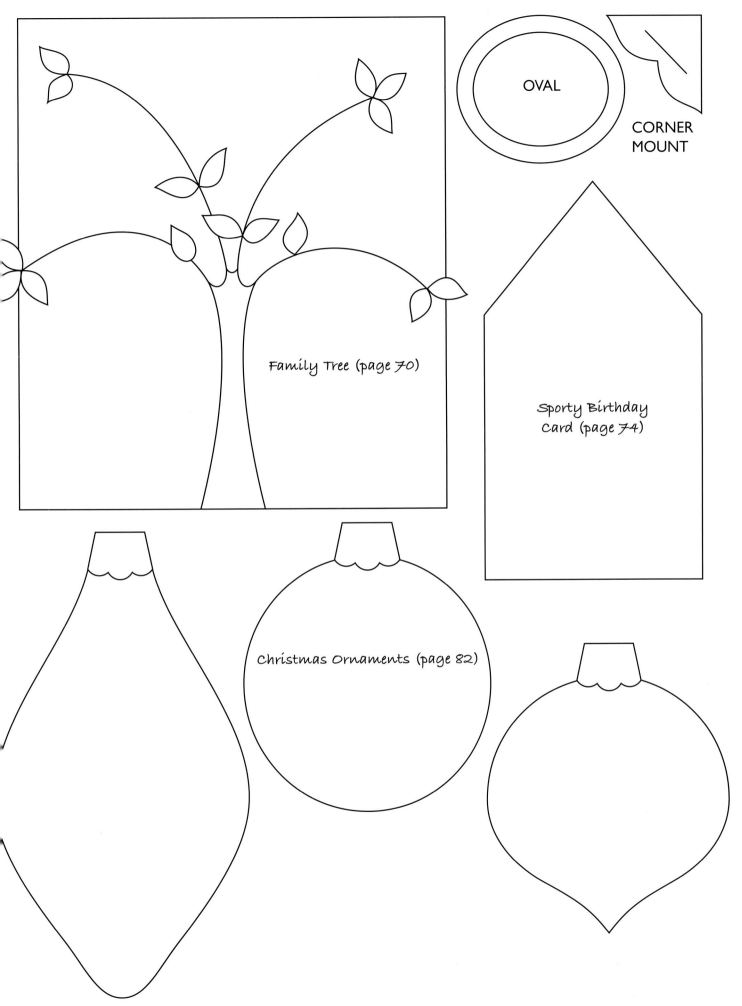

OVAL

CORNER
MOUNT

Family Tree (page 70)

Sporty Birthday
Card (page 74)

Christmas Ornaments (page 82)

Resource List

Achiver's Inc. – The Photo Memory Store

www. archiversonline.com

Cartwright's Sequins

www.cartwright.com

Sequins

DecoArt Inc.

www.decoart.com

Acrylic paint

Delta Technical Coating, Inc.

www.deltacrafts.com

Acrylic paint

Hobby Lobby Creative Centers

www.hobbylobby.com

Impress

www.impressrubberstamps.com

Rubber stamps

Jo-Ann Fabric & Crafts

www.JoAnn.com

Kate's Paperie

www.katespaperie.com

Cardstock; patterned and textured papers

Michaels – The Arts and Crafts Store

www.michaels.com

Thermo O Web

www.thermoweb.com

Adhesives

Two Peas in a Bucket

www.twopeasinabucket.com

Adhesives, cardstock, papers, stickers

index

New and Bestselling Titles from

America's Best-Loved Craft & Hobby Books®
America's Best-Loved Knitting Books®

America's Best-Loved Quilt Books®

NEW RELEASES
Alphabet Soup
Big Knitting
Big 'n Easy
Courtship Quilts
Crazy Eights
Creating Your Perfect Quilting
   Space
Crochet from the Heart
Fabulous Flowers
First Crochet
Fun and Funky Crochet
Joined at the Heart
Little Box of Knitted Ponchos and
   Wraps, The
Little Box of Knitted Throws, The
Merry Christmas Quilts
More Crocheted Aran Sweaters
Party Time!
Perfectly Brilliant Knits
Polka-Dot Kids' Quilts
Quilt Block Bonanza
Quilts from Grandmother's Garden
Raise the Roof
Saturday Sweaters
Save the Scraps

**Our books are available
at bookstores and your favorite
craft, fabric,
and yarn retailers.
If you don't see
the title you're
looking for, visit us at
www.martingale-pub.com
or contact us at:**

1-800-426-3126

International: 1-425-483-3313
Fax: 1-425-486-7596
Email: info@martingale-pub.com

Seeing Stars
Sensational Knitted Socks
Sensational Sashiko
Strip-Pieced Quilts
Tea in the Garden
Treasury of Scrap Quilts, A

LEARNING TO QUILT
101 Fabulous Rotary-Cut Quilts
Happy Endings, Revised Edition
Loving Stitches, Revised Edition
Magic of Quiltmaking, The
Quilter's Quick Reference Guide,
   The
Sensational Settings, Revised
   Edition
Your First Quilt Book (or it should
   be!)

QUILTS FOR BABIES & CHILDREN
American Doll Quilts
Even More Quilts for Baby
More Quilts for Baby
Quilts for Baby
Sweet and Simple Baby Quilts

SCRAP QUILTS
More Nickel Quilts
Nickel Quilts
Scrap Frenzy
Successful Scrap Quilts

TOPICS IN QUILTMAKING
Basket Bonanza
Cottage-Style Quilts
Everyday Folk Art
Focus on Florals
Follow the Dots . . . to Dazzling
   Quilts
Log Cabin Quilts
More Biblical Quilt Blocks
Quilter's Home: Spring, The
Scatter Garden Quilts

Shortcut to Drunkard's Path, A
Strawberry Fair
Summertime Quilts
Tried and True
Warm Up to Wool

CRAFTS
Bag Boutique
Collage Cards
Creating with Paint
Painted Fabric Fun
Purely Primitive
Stamp in Color
Trashformations
Vintage Workshop, The: Gifts for
   All Occasions
Year of Cats...in Hats!, A

KNITTING & CROCHET
200 Knitted Blocks
365 Knitting Stitches a Year:
   Perpetual Calendar
Classic Crocheted Vests
Crocheted Socks!
Dazzling Knits
First Knits
Handknit Style
Knitted Throws and More for the
   Simply Beautiful Home
Knitting with Hand-Dyed Yarns
Little Box of Crocheted Hats and
   Scarves, The
Little Box of Scarves, The
Little Box of Scarves II, The
Little Box of Sweaters, The
Pleasures of Knitting, The
Pursenalities
Rainbow Knits for Kids
Sarah Dallas Knitting
Ultimate Knitted Tee, The